Go Wild! in the Lake District

Text: *Vivienne Crow*
Series editor: *Tony Bowerman*
Photographs: *Paula Thanner, Vivienne Crow, Adobe Stock, Alamy, Dreamstime, Shutterstock*
Design: *Laura Hodgkinson | laurahodgkinson.com*

© Northern Eye Books Limited 2021

Vivienne Crow has asserted her rights under the Copyright, Designs and Patents Act, 1988 to be identified as the author of this work. All rights reserved.

This book contains mapping data licensed from the Ordnance Survey with the permission of the Controller of Her Majesty's Stationery Office. © Crown copyright 2021. All rights reserved. License number 100047867

Northern Eye Books
ISBN 978-1-908632-94-4

A CIP catalogue record for this book is available from the British Library.

www.northerneyebooks.co.uk

Important Advice: The routes described in this book are undertaken at the reader's own risk. Walkers should take into account their level of fitness, wear suitable footwear and clothing, and carry food and water. It is also advisable to take the relevant OS map with you in case you get lost and leave the area covered by our maps.

Whilst every care has been taken to ensure the accuracy of the route directions, the publishers cannot accept responsibility for errors or omissions, or for changes in the details given. Nor can the publisher and copyright owners accept responsibility for any consequences arising from the use of this book.

If you find any inaccuracies in either the text or maps, please write or email us at the address below. Thank you.

First published in 2021 by
Northern Eye Books Limited
Northern Eye Books, Tattenhall, Cheshire CH3 9PX
tony@northerneyebooks.co.uk
www.northerneyebooks.co.uk

@northerneyebooks
@northerneyeboo

For sales enquiries, please call 01928 723 744

Cover: *Forest fun (Adventure 10)*

Contents

Go Wild! in the Lake District 4

Top 10 family adventures 6

Before you set off 8

What to take 10

1 Binsey Hillbagging – *summit sunset* 12

2 St Herbert's Island – *paddle and picnic* .. 18

3 Hallin Fell – *'steamer' trip and climb* 24

4 Crummock Water – *wild swim* 30

5 Buttermere – *lake walk (with tunnel)* 36

6 Black Sail Hut – *bike and bunk* 42

7 Cathedral Cave – *caves scramble* 48

8 Stanley Ghyll – *steam train & waterfall* .. 56

9 Windermere Shore – *boat and bike* 64

10 Grizedale Forest – *mountain biking* 70

Useful Information 76

Go Wild! in the Lake District

THE LAKE DISTRICT NATIONAL PARK is the largest and most popular of the thirteen National Parks in England and Wales. Created as one of Britain's first National Parks in 1951, its role is to 'conserve and enhance' the natural beauty, wildlife and culture of this iconic English landscape — both for residents and visitors today, and for future generations.

Wordsworth described the English Lake District, in his 1810 *Guide to the Lakes*, as a 'sort of national property in which every man has a right and interest who has an eye to perceive and a heart to enjoy'. Today, the Park's 912 square miles embrace dramatic fells and dales, more than 400 lakes and tarns and eight National Nature Reserves — all publicly accessible on nearly 2,000 miles of footpaths and other rights of way. The Lake District is a much-loved and cherished landscape. It's no surprise that it attracts an estimated 24 million day visitors a year.

Amazing adventures

Hills and lakes, caves and forests, boats and trains… The Lake District is packed with natural and man-made features that make it one of the biggest and best outdoor playgrounds in the country.

There's loads of fun to be had from messing about in the great outdoors, and families can share all sorts of adventures in this dramatic landscape. While children of all ages walk, bike, swim and canoe their way around the National Park, they'll experience a growing sense of achievement — a big boost to their confidence. But it's not just about the kids: parents will enjoy these days out too, revelling in the chance to indulge their 'inner child' and get back to nature.

> "Little People,
> Growing shoots.
> Happy hearts,
> Muddy boots."

Penny Whitehouse

Top 10 family adventures

THESE ARE THE LAKE DISTRICT'S ten best **family adventures**, providing some wonderful days out for children and adults alike. They cover all sorts of activities, including traffic-free bike rides, short hill walks, wild swims, scrambling, cave exploration, canoeing, trips on boats and steam trains, a visit to a hidden waterfall and even an overnight stay in one of England's remotest hostels. And, for each adventure, there's a series of suggested challenges to help families get the most out of their special time in the Lakes.

1 Sunset Picnic — page 12

2 Island Paddle — page 18

3 Hilltop View — page 24

4 Wild Swim — page 30

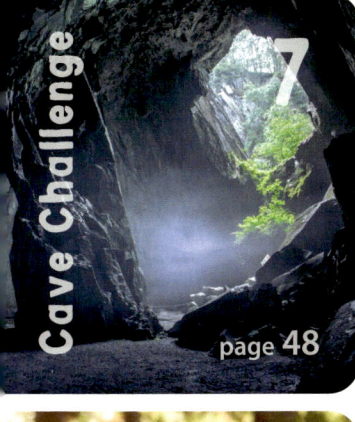

Lake + Tunnel — 5 page 36	**Bike + Bunk** — 6 page 42
Cave Challenge — 7 page 48	**Train + Waterfall** — 8 page 56
Ferry + Cycle — 9 page 64	**Forest Biking** — 10 page 70

Before you set off ...

ANY OUTDOOR ADVENTURE requires some planning, whether it's a trek to the North Pole or a short walk beside a lake. Having the kit you need and knowing how to use it, being prepared for whatever the weather might throw at you, carrying enough food and drink — get these things right and you've taken the first step to a great day out for young and old alike.

Choosing the right adventure

The activities in this book include walks, bike rides, wild swims, canoeing, scrambling and an overnight stay in a remote hostel. Each chapter has a page describing what you can expect, the level of difficulty, suitability for different age groups and a list of some of the things you'll need to take with you. Read these to help decide what your family's likely to enjoy.

Watch the weather

Check a reliable local forecast before you set off. There's no point going up Binsey or Hallin Fell if it's misty on the fell-tops and, likewise, you're not going to want to go cycling if there's a gale blowing. Remember as well to always take warm, waterproof clothing with you — just in case the weather changes — as well as sun protection.

Food and drink

The more energy you're using up, the more food you'll need, so pack plenty to keep everyone going. (Don't forget any pets, too.) Water or soft drinks are important — not just in hot weather — and, if you're going for a swim or a paddle, think about taking a flask of hot chocolate or something similar to help everyone warm up afterwards.

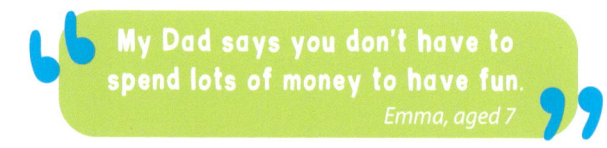

> **My Dad says you don't have to spend lots of money to have fun.**
> *Emma, aged 7*

Making memories

If things go wrong...

If your children are getting tired or the weather suddenly takes an unexpected turn for the worse, it might be a wise idea to turn back. You can always try again another day.

Kids being kids, they will hurt themselves from time to time. Grazed knees can be remedied with plasters or sometimes just a cuddle but, in the event of a real emergency, don't hesitate to call 999.

Be #AdventureSmart!

Before you head out for the day with your family, ask yourself three questions…

Do I know what the weather will be like?
Do I have the right gear?
Do I have the knowledge and skills for the day?

If you answer 'yes' to these questions, off you go!
If not, choose an alternative or wait for better weather.

What to take

COMFORT IS THE KEY when deciding what to wear and what to take. It's always advisable to have warm and waterproof clothing with you, even if it never gets used. Jeans are probably not a good idea – if they get wet, they'll take ages to dry and leave the wearer feeling cold. Choose footwear suitable for the activity. As well as food and drink, consider packing a small first aid kit in case of cuts and grazes. There are more suggestions below as well as a tailored list at the start of each chapter.

Walking

For walking Lakeland paths, footwear with good grip and ankle support is recommended. You won't experience any serious navigational challenges on any of the routes in this book, but you will need to know how to use a map and compass. Don't forget to pack a torch too, especially where there are tunnels along the route and for walking late in the day.

Cycling

If you're bringing your own gear, don't forget you'll need helmets and bike lights. It's also advisable to fit bikes with bells to warn others on shared-use paths. Most bike hire outfits provide all the kit you need, but confirm this when booking. Some companies hire out tag-alongs, trailers and bike seats for younger, less experienced cyclists.

Canoeing/kayaking

Keeping feet dry, especially when getting in and out of canoes and kayaks, is virtually impossible, so water shoes or sandals are recommended. Everyone will also need life jackets or, for stronger swimmers, buoyancy aids. Most hire companies will provide these, but check before booking. Carry valuables and spare clothes in a dry bag.

> **Mum took enough food for a week!**
> *Faisal, aged 8*

In the swing of things

Swimming

Water shoes or sandals are good for protecting feet when getting in and out of the lake. Consider investing in wetsuits to prevent children from getting too cold. There's no need to splash out – if you'll excuse the pun – you can get fairly basic kids' wetsuits for about £20. Don't forget towels too, and some warm clothes for when you get out of the water.

Overnight gear

For the Black Sail Hut trip (*adventure 6*), you'll need the things you'd normally pack for a night away from home, including PJs and toothbrush. Bike panniers are ideal for carrying your gear. Don't forget a torch and some cash (the hostel doesn't have card facilities). Bedding is provided and towel hire is available. Meals can be booked, although there is a self-catering kitchen if you want to keep costs down.

12 ♦ **Go Wild! In the Lake District**

Cuddle break

Summit cairn

"Dad went `Wow!' My sunset photos went viral"

#LakeDistrictFells
#GoWildLakeDistrict
#LakeDistrictNationalPark

Sunset over the sea

adventure 1

Hill yomp and a sunset snack

Walk to Binsey hill-top, on the edge of Lakeland, to watch the sun set over the sea

Start: Small parking area near Binsey Lodge, close to High Bewaldeth. OS grid ref: NY 235 350. *From the Castle Inn on the A591 near Bassenthwaite, take the minor road heading north-east towards Uldale and Caldbeck. After 3.2 kilometres (2 miles), take the second turning on the left – towards Ireby. Take the next left and the parking area is just on your right*

Map: Ordnance Survey Explorer OL4 (1:25,000), The Lake District: North-western area, *Keswick, Cockermouth & Wigton*

You'll love this if... You enjoy being on the hills when everyone else has gone home and the light's at its most magical

How far is it? 1¾ miles/2.7 kilometres

How long does it take? Summer evening adventure. Allow about two hours for the walk (there and back), plus extra time to eat and explore

You'll need: Suitable footwear and clothes (it gets colder as the sun goes down); a picnic; map and compass

What's more: Take a headtorch to help light your way as you head back down

Grub's up: Snooty Fox pub and Mae's Tea Rooms and Gallery in Uldale; Emily's Black Lion pub, Ireby

What's it like?

Incy-wincy Binsey is right on the northern edge of the Lake District. It's not very high but, because there are no other big hills between this one and the coast, it's a great place to watch the sun set over the sea. There's a fairly steep climb, but once you're at the top, you can enjoy an evening picnic with the birds singing all around. On the way back, keep your eyes peeled for creatures that only come out at twilight, such as badgers and bats.

Grade:
Easy/Moderate

Suitable for:
Families with children capable of a walk up a small, but steep-sided grassy hill; paths unsuitable for pushchairs

Taking a breather

No problem!

Route in a nutshell

Broad, grassy path all the way from road to summit – moderately steep all the way – a few damp bits of ground, but generally good underfoot – bouldery summit area – return to road on same path

ALONG THE WAY

Fill in each activity on the next page!

- Skill test
- Nature detective
- I spy
- Cheeky challenge

Skill test: Find Skiddaw, and then use your compass to work out which direction it is.

② Keep to the clearest path as you walk steadily uphill, ignoring a branch trail to the left fairly early on.

In spring and early summer, the sky above these grassy slopes is filled with the song of skylarks, one of the chirpiest birds you'll hear on the hills. It's only a small bird, but it makes a lot of noise! If you've got a dog, it's important to keep it on a lead as skylarks nest on the ground rather than in trees.

Let's go!

① Go through the small, **wooden gate** at the south-western end of the parking area. (The end furthest from the road junction.)

Once you've stepped across a **tiny stream** close to the gate, you'll see a fairly clear, **grassy path** heading uphill, straight ahead. Follow this. It soon bends left, passing a small group of twisted, old hawthorn trees on the right.

In spring, these will be covered with white flowers sometimes known as May blossom because that's the month when they usually appear.

③ As you approach the **first cairn** on the **summit** area, ignore another path to the left. Keeping right here, you'll quickly step up on to the summit area. The first thing you'll see is a simple **cairn**, followed by a **trig pillar** and then a collection of **stone shelters**.

The boulders here are the remains of a 'tumulus' which prehistoric people would've used as burial place – like a cemetery.

Adventure 1 | Binsey Hillbagging ♦ 15

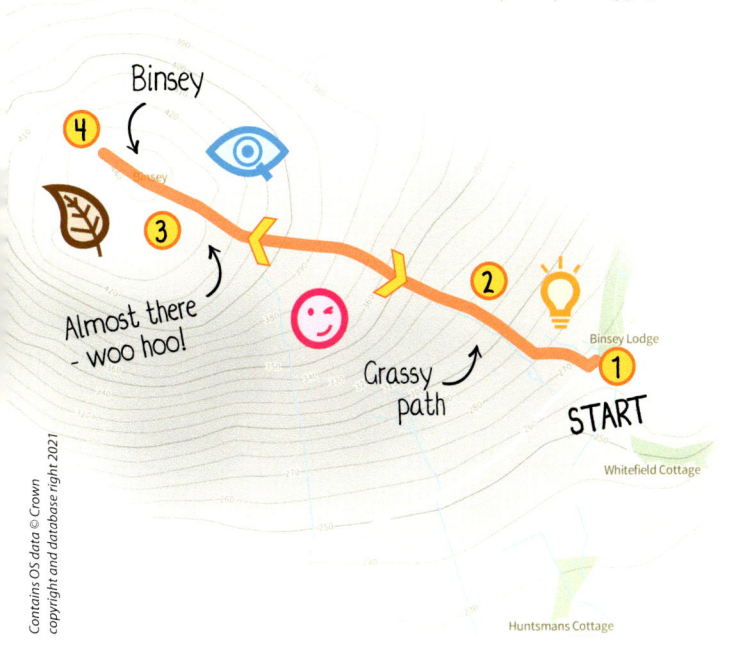

Contains OS data © Crown copyright and database right 2021

Nature detective: Look for the biggest patch of lichen you can find on the rocks.

You can sit and have your picnic anywhere, but the **best view** of the coast – and the best place to watch the sun going down – is from the **cairn** at the furthest (north-western) end of the summit area.

I spy: Count the number of wind turbines you can see from the cairn.

④ After the sun's disappeared, return to the **trig pillar** and then the **first cairn** you reached on the summit area. Now **retrace your steps** to the parking area.

Cheeky challenge: Watch for a good place to do a roly-poly as you head downhill.

As it starts getting darker, you might need to use a torch.
Keep your eyes peeled for creatures that are more active at this time of the day – animals such as foxes, badgers and deer. You might even hear an owl. ♦

Skill test
Which way's Skiddaw?

Where the path bends left near the hawthorn trees, look to the left and you'll see a **big mountain** looming over the countryside. This is **Skiddaw**, England's fourth highest mountain.

Use your compass to work out which direction this is from the hawthorn trees. If **Skiddaw's** disappeared in the low cloud, you might need to use a map to find it.

Map and compass

Tick your response

○ North   ○ South   ○ Couldn't find it

Nature detective
Lichen hunt

Many of the rocks on Binsey's summit look like they're covered in paint splotches. It's not paint though; it's **lichen**, an organism that grows on stones, trees, even roof tiles.

The bigger the **lichen**, the older it is. Some of the **lichen** on Binsey might be hundreds of years old. Find the biggest patch you can.

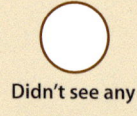

Liking lichen?

Tick your response

○ Didn't see any   ○ Found one as big as a doughnut   ○ Saw one the size of a dinner plate

👁 I spy
Trapped wind?

The west coast of Britain, including Cumbria, has lots of **wind turbines** because it gets a lot of **windy weather**. If you look out to the coast from the top of Binsey, there are several groups of them. You'll even see a **big wind farm** out to sea.

How many **wind turbines** you can count from the summit?

Wind farm

Tick your response

- Only saw four or five
- About 25
- Loads and loads out at sea

😉 Cheeky challenge
Roly-poly time!

When you're coming back down Binsey, the grassy path is ideal for **rolling down**. Are you brave enough to attempt a **roly-poly**?

You'll need to find a slope that doesn't have any stones sticking out of it; otherwise you could hurt yourself. Ask an adult to catch you at the bottom.

Downhill dizzy

Tick your response

- I feel sick!
- Total doddle
- Chickened out

#LakeDistrictAdventures
#GoWildLakeDistrict
#LakeDistrictLakes

"It was magical on the water. What an amazing day!"

St Herbert's Island

Wet and wild

Happy chappy

adventure 2

Epic paddle to a wild island

Cross beautiful Derwentwater in a kayak or canoe to explore a mysterious island

Start: Nichol End Marine, Portinscale, near Keswick. OS grid ref: NY 254 228. Kayaks and canoes can also be hired/launched from Derwentwater Marina, also in Portinscale

Map: Ordnance Survey Explorer OL4 (1:25,000), The Lake District: North-western area, *Keswick, Cockermouth & Wigton*

You'll love this if... You like messing about on boats and have always dreamed of being on a desert island

How far is it? 2 miles/3.2 kilometres (there and back, if you paddle in a straight line)

How long does it take? Half-day adventure. Assuming you spend 40 minutes on the island, allow at least two hours for the entire adventure, more if it's windy

You'll need: If you're hiring equipment, buoyancy aids/life jackets are provided, but bring dry clothes in case you get wet; food and drink; water shoes/sandals; map and compass

What's more: Private vessels can be launched from other sites, including Kettlewell car park (NY 266 195)

Grub's up: Café at Nichol End Marine

More info: Nichol End Marine, 017687 73082, **www.nicholend.co.uk**; Derwentwater Marina, 017687 72912, **www.derwentwatermarina.co.uk**

What's it like?

Following in the wake of Beatrix Potter's Squirrel Nutkin and his friends, paddling across Derwentwater is a wonderful experience. Gazing up at the surrounding fells from the water gives lake users a fresh perspective on the area – and a peaceful one, thanks to the absence of power boats. The destination is St Herbert's Island, just 300 metres from tip to toe – home to ruins and lots of potential picnic spots. For easy paddling, save this for a calm day.

Grade: *Moderate*

Suitable for: *Families with children who can be trusted around water and are strong enough for paddling*

Paddle power

Hi Dad - 'Over'

Route in a nutshell

Paddle across lake for about 1 mile (allow extra time if there's even a slight breeze) – land on shingle beach – explore island – picnic – paddle back across lake

ALONG THE WAY

Skill test ....

Nature detective ....

I spy ....

Cheeky challenge ....

Fill in each activity on the next page!

Let's go!

① As you paddle away from the **Nichol End Marine at Portinscale**, aim initially for the wooded, egg-shaped island to the south-east. This is **Derwent Isle**, the only inhabited island on the lake.

Members of the public are not allowed to land, but you'll get a good view of it as you make your way across the water. You'll also be able to see the steep, wooded slopes of Walla Crag beyond Derwent Isle on the far side of the lake.

② After about 300 metres, veer south-south-east, now aiming for the northern tip of **St Herbert's Island**. *In Beatrix Potter's book, The Tale of Squirrel Nutkin, the fluffy-tailed hero of the book and some of his red squirrel chums paddle out to the island on tiny rafts. In the book, St Herbert's is called Owl Island, and it's home to an owl known as Old Brown.*

> **Nature detective**: Stop paddling for a few minutes and see if you can spot any underwater creatures.

③ Nearing the island, you'll see a **narrow, shingle spit** at its northern tip. Just south of this, on the western shore, is a **stony beach**. Big enough to land several boats on, this is probably the easiest place to aim for if you're coming at the island from Portinscale or Keswick, although there are lots of other landing spots on the eastern side too.

④ Having pulled your boats out of the water and on to the beach, you can wander wherever you want on the island – there are no restrictions.

There are trees to climb and plenty of places to play hide and seek. More than 1,300 years ago, this island became the

Adventure 2 | St Herbert's Island ♦ 21

lonely home of a priest, St Herbert, who decided to live apart from other people and spend much of his life praying. There are no signs today of the simple hermitage in which he lived, although there are the remains of another building, possibly from Victorian times, that may have been built on the site of a medieval chapel.

I spy: Explore the island and see if you can find the hidden ruins.

Skill test: Gather materials and make a tiny boat or a raft, like the one Squirrel Nutkin used.

After your picnic, make your way back across the lake, remembering to head **north-north-west** for much of the time. Only as you near **Portinscale**, should you swing to the north-west.

This time, the views are dominated by Skiddaw, the massive mountain straight ahead. This is the fourth's highest mountain in England, after Scafell Pike, Scafell and Helvellyn. ♦

Cheeky challenge: On your way back across Derwentwater, try paddling in as tight a circle as you can.

---

① START
②
Ahoy there! Not far now!
③
④
Mysterious island

Contains OS data © Crown copyright and database right 2021

🍃 Nature detective
Something fishy...

Once you're **out on the water**, look around to check you're not going to be in anyone's way and, if it's safe to do so, stop paddling.

While trying to keep the vessel as still as possible, look into the lake and see if you can spot any **fish** – or any other **water creatures**.

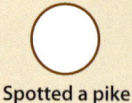

Minnows

○ Tick your response

○ Saw some small fish

○ Spotted a pike

○ Wow, the Loch Ness Monster!

👁 I spy
The lost building

Explore the island and see if you can find the **remains of a building**. Little more than **a few stones**, it's camouflaged by all the vegetation and you have to look hard to find it.

To help you... It's hidden among the trees less than 100 metres south of the shingle beach you landed on.

Woodland hunt

○ Tick your response

○ Found it!

○ Not sure; found a few stones

○ Looked, but no luck

💡 Skill test
Make a tiny boat

While you're exploring the island, gather up materials such as sticks and leaves. When you get back to the beach for your picnic, use them to make a **tiny boat**.

You probably won't manage anything sturdy enough to carry Squirrel Nutkin or his friends, but see how long it'll **float** for on the lake.

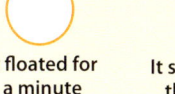

Bark boat

Tick your response

○ Mine sank!   ○ It floated for a minute   ○ It sailed off into the distance

😉 Cheeky challenge
Going round in circles

Now you're more used to **paddling**, test your new-found abilities on your way back to the shore. As before, look around to check you're not in anyone's way and, if it's safe, try **paddling in a circle**.

Keep the **circle as small as possible**. It's not as easy as you might think!

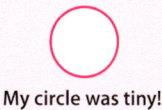

Kayak skills?

Tick your response

○ My circle was tiny!   ○ I fell in   ○ Does a straight line count?

24 ♦ Go Wild! In the Lake District

Me and Dad

On the ferry

"You can see for miles down the lake."

View down Ullswater

#FellWalking
#GoWildLakeDistrict
#WainwrightBagging

adventure 3

Boat trip to a busting view

Ullswater boat trip to climb a cairn-topped hill with panoramic views of lake and fells

Start: Howtown's pier. OS grid ref: NY 443 199. Catch Ullswater 'Steamer' from Glenridding or Pooley Bridge

Map: Ordnance Survey Explorer OL5 (1:25,000), The Lake District: North-eastern area, *Penrith, Patterdale & Caldbeck*

You'll love this if... You adore the water, you adore the hills and you think the two combined are the best thing

How far is it? 2½ miles/4 kilometres

How long does it take? Half-day adventure. Allow at least two hours for the walk, plus extra time to eat and play

You'll need: Some money to pay for the boat; suitable clothes and footwear; a picnic; map and compass

What's more: Even on a warm summer's day, you'll need an extra layer or two for the boat trip

Grub's up: Howtown Hotel and Tearoom; pubs and cafés in Pooley Bridge and Glenridding

More info: Details of Ullswater 'Steamer' fares and timetables at **www.ullswater-steamers.co.uk** or 017684 82229

What's it like?

Would-be fell-walkers will love climbing this little fell and bagging one of their first Wainwrights. At just 388m/1,273ft, Hallin Fell is one of the smallest hills classified as a Wainwright and yet it feels much bigger as you puff and pant your way to the top and then gaze out along Ullswater to some of England's highest mountains. And it all starts and ends with a boat trip along the lake. What could be better?

Grade:
Moderate

Suitable for:
Families with children capable of a walk up a small, but steep-sided grassy hill; paths unsuitable for pushchairs

Howtown ferry

Heading up

Route in a nutshell

Lakeside path – lane – set of rough steps – good path along base of fell – steep, grassy paths leading to summit – steep, grassy path dropping from summit – short section on quiet road – retrace steps along base of fell

ALONG THE WAY

Skill test

Nature detective

I spy

Cheeky challenge

Fill in each activity on the next page!

Let's go!

Nature detective: While you're on the boat, watch for mute swans on the lake.

① Get off the 'steamer' at **Howtown** and turn right beyond the **pier**. Go right again along a lane and then through a gate on the left.

② At the top of some **steps**, go through another gate and turn left. Keep right when the path forks.

③ Just before the road, take the trail uphill on the right. When you reach a flat, **concrete construction**, turn right (north-north-east), climbing more steeply. Having ignored an easy-to-miss trail to the left early on, watch carefully for the point at which the path bends left. (Another, narrower path keeps straight on here.)

I spy: Count the total number of cairns you see on the walk.

④ Make your way up to a **large cairn**. Keep right (north) at a clear fork and then go straight over a path crossing. You can now see the top of Hallin Fell to the left. You've already climbed a fair bit from the lake, but there's still some way to go. And, as you near the summit, the ground gets rockier. It may only be a tiddler, but it's a proper mountain!

There are a couple of **knolls** (small hills) on the right soon, providing good views over Ullswater. You can climb them if you want; otherwise, keep left at two forks in quick succession. At the next fork though – on potentially soggy ground

Adventure 3 | Hallin Fell | 27

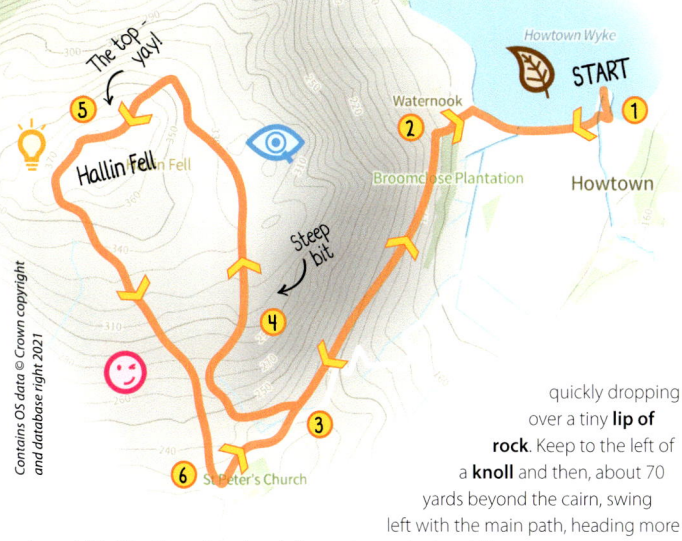

– bear right. After the path swings left, it climbs through a **shallow gully** with rocks sticking out either side. (Watch for another **cairn** to the right of the path.)

5 When you finally reach the sturdy **cairn** on **Hallin Fell's summit**, give yourself a big pat on the back – you've climbed one of the 214 hills in the Lake District known as 'Wainwrights'. You can see a lot of other Wainwrights from here.

> **Skill test:** Use your map and compass to work out which of them is Helvellyn.

From the **cairn**, walk in roughly the same direction as before (south-west), quickly dropping over a tiny **lip of rock**. Keep to the left of a **knoll** and then, about 70 yards beyond the cairn, swing left with the main path, heading more steeply downhill.

> **Cheeky challenge:** Once you're past any rocky bits, look out for a good place to walk barefoot.

Keep to the clearest path and it'll eventually drop you on to a **quiet lane**.

6 Turn left here. Just before the lane starts heading steeply downhill, take the **stony path** on the left. Almost immediately, you'll step over a **tiny stream** (sometimes dry in summer). You should now recognise this as the path you left at waypoint 3. Retrace your steps to the **pier**. ♦

🍃 Nature detective
Swan, two, three...

While on the boat, look out for **mute swans**. These huge white birds have long necks that enable them to search for food under the water. They love eating plants that live in the lake as well as small fish and even frogs.

Some people feed bread to **swans** but it can make them ill, so it's best not to. How many **swans** can you see?

Mute swans

Tick your response

○ Hundreds!   ○ Spotted one or two   ○ Saw some ducks

👁 I spy
Cairn you count them?

Cairns are the piles of stones that help mark the route of paths on the hills. They stop people straying and getting lost. The tops of most Lake District hills will have cairns marking their summits too. The one on Hallin Fell is particularly well-built.

How many **cairns** you can count on this walk?

Summit cairn

Tick your response

○ Twenty-four   ○ Spotted 1 or 2   ○ I counted 8

💡 Skill test
Where's Helvellyn?

Did you know that you can see England's third highest mountain, **Helvellyn**, from the top of Hallin Fell? Use your **map and compass** to work out which one it is while you're having your picnic. You need to be looking south-west to find it.

In winter, you'll find mountaineers, ice-climbers and even skiers on **Helvellyn**.

Map and compass

Tick your response

○ Found it!   ○ Took me four minutes   ○ It's much too foggy

😉 Cheeky challenge
Going barefoot

When you're coming down Hallin Fell, there are some smooth, grassy slopes ideal for **walking barefoot**. Take your **shoes and socks off** and give it a try! (Just make sure there's nothing nasty on the ground first though.)

It's a nice feeling, isn't it? Some studies have shown that walking barefoot every now and then can be good for us too.

Tickle your toes

Tick your response

○ Felt nice!   ○ It tickles   ○ Kept my shoes on!

30 ♦ Go Wild! In the Lake District

"Clear water, pebble beach, stunning views. What more could you want?"

#WildSwimming
#GoWildLakeDistrict
#WildSwimmingLakeDistrict

Swimming in Crummock Water

Emerging from the depths

Ducking and diving

adventure 4

Wild swim in a cool lake

Stroll to Crummock Water's beaches for a cool wild swim, surrounded by mountains

Start: Lake District National Park car park behind the Bridge Hotel in Buttermere. OS grid ref: NY 174 169

Map: Ordnance Survey Explorer OL4 (1:25,000), The Lake District: North-western area, *Keswick, Cockermouth & Wigton*

You'll love this if... You want to swim outdoors with rugged mountains towering over you

How far is it? The walk is 1½ mile/2.5 kilometres (there and back)

How long does it take? Half-day adventure. Allow 45 minutes for the return walk, plus time for getting changed, swimming and drying off

You'll need: Map; swimming gear (preferably wet suit and water shoes/sandals); towel; warm layers

What's more: Competent adult swimmers should check the depth and temperature of the water first …and supervise children at all times

Grub's up: Croft House Café, Syke Farm Tearoom, Bridge Hotel and Buttermere Court Hotel, all in Buttermere

More info: Unless you're used to it, you'll find outdoor swimming harder than swimming in a warm pool. However hot the weather, the water in lakes is always cold. For more advice, visit **www.outdoorswimmingsociety.com** or **www.wildswimming.co.uk**

Grade:
Easy/Moderate

Suitable for:
Families with children who swim well and can be trusted around water

Fun for all the family

Cheeky squirrel

What's it like?

The adventure starts with a gorgeous walk from the village of Buttermere – partly beside a beck, partly through woodland – and then gets even better. Stepping from the beach into the blue of Crummock Water for a swim is like leaving the everyday world behind. Above, you've got the fells and the sky; below are the unknown depths. For adults and children alike, it's simultaneously fun, exciting and liberating.

32 ♦ Go Wild! In the Lake District

Route in a nutshell

Walk across meadows beside beck – up and over wooded knoll – lakeshore – entry to lake from gently shelving, stony beach – wild swim – retrace walk along shore and beside beck

Fill in each activity on the next page!

ALONG THE WAY

Skill test ....
Nature detective ....
I spy ....
Cheeky challenge ....

Let's go!

① Walk to the far end of the **car park**, away from the vehicle entrance. Ignoring the large gates, go through a small **wooden gate** over to the right. This provides access to a **beckside path**. Don't be tempted by the bridge leading into the campsite early on; instead keep the beck on your right. When the fenced section of path ends, go through the **pedestrian gate** and continue beside the **beck** down the side of a field. This part of the route can be a bit wet and muddy at times.

I spy: This field often has sheep and cattle in it. See how many Herdies you can count.

② Ignoring the next bridge, keep following the line of the fenced **beck downstream**. As you enter a small patch of **woodland**, a trail goes up and over the shoulder of this **knoll**. As you come down the other side, you reach the first **shingle beach** beside **Crummock Water**. The bed of the lake shelves away quite steeply here, so it's not ideal for swimming, but it is a lovely spot to enjoy the lake and the fells rising up from its shores. The hill directly opposite is **Melbreak**, while the low ridge to the north is **Rannerdale Knotts**.

Skill test: Who can skim a stone furthest on the lake? Or make it bounce the most?

(The next section is sometimes closed to the public while sandpipers nest on the shore. Please heed the notices.)

Adventure 4 | Crummock Water | 33

Contains OS data © Crown copyright and database right 2021

③ Turn right, through the kissing-gate, and immediately bear half-right across a **grassy area** to find the **footbridge** over the beck you followed down from the car park. Now head **back to the shore** and continue north. The **beach** here is much better for swimming.

④ Alternatively, you can continue to the **next beach**. To do so, continue in the same direction, through the **gate** and over a **small bridge**. Bear left at a fork to keep to the gorgeous lakeshore path through the trees. This is a little rough and rocky in places. Leaving the **woods** via **another gate**, head straight back to the **water's edge**. Cross one **final beck** via a **small stone bridge**. The lake can be entered almost anywhere between here and the small stand of pine trees near the base of the fell. This **grassy area** is also good for picnics.

> **Cheeky challenge**: While you're in the water, find the roundest pebble you can on the bed of the lake.

⑤ Once you've enjoyed your swim in the lake, retrace your steps back to the car park in **Buttermere village**. ♦

> **Nature detective**: Listen for buzzards. Their calls are a bit like a cat mewing, but higher pitched.

👁 I spy
Happy Herdies

Herdwicks, affectionately known as 'Herdies', are a local breed of **sheep** that are particularly suited to the Lake District's harsh weather.

The lambs are born black and get lighter as they grow older. The adult sheep can be identified from their grey wool and the fact that they always seem to have a **smile** on their faces.

Herdwick sheep

Tick your response

○ I counted 10   ○ Lost count!   ○ I only saw cows

💡 Skill test
Skimming stones

Find a **flat stone** and hold it between your thumb and forefinger, resting it on your middle finger. Pull your wrist back and flick the stone away from you.

Don't throw it up into the air – instead, bend slightly to get as **low** to the water as you can, and launch it directly on to the water's surface. How many times can you **bounce** it?

Skimming stones

Tick your response

○ Mine bounced once   ○ I managed four bounces   ○ No bounces for me!

😉 Cheeky challenge
In deep

While you're in the shallow water, try to find the roundest, **smoothest** pebble you can on the bed of the lake.

The best way to do this is to keep your eyes **open** while putting your head under the water. If you find this too scary though, simply try feeling for **pebbles** with your fingertips.

Lake pebbles

Tick your response

◯ I found one like a golf ball
◯ My best one was egg-shaped
◯ I found loads!

🍃 Nature detective
Buzzards on call

Buzzards are among the largest and most common birds of prey in the UK. They can be found anywhere from flat farmland and **woodland** to rugged **mountainous** terrain.

Listen for their high-pitched '**mewing**' calls or watch for pairs soaring high in the sky. You might also be lucky enough to see one perched on a tree or **fencepost**.

Buzzard

Tick your response

◯ I thought I heard one
◯ I only heard the sheep
◯ I saw two buzzards circling

36 ♦ Go Wild! In the Lake District

#Buttermere
#GoWildLakeDistrict
#LakeDistrictUK

"What a beautiful lake. The kids loved the rocky tunnel half way round."

Buttermere pines

Round the lake

Spooky tunnel

adventure 5

Lakeside loop & spooky tunnel

Walk round beautiful Buttermere with a trip through a dripping rock-cut tunnel

Start: Lake District National Park car park behind the Bridge Hotel in Buttermere. OS grid ref: NY 174 169

Map: Ordnance Survey Explorer OL4 (1:25,000), The Lake District: North-western area, *Keswick, Cockermouth & Wigton*

You'll love this if... You love walking where the lakes meet the mountains – and enjoy spooky tunnels!

How far is it? 5 miles/8 kilometres

How long does it take? Half-day adventure. Allow two to three hours for the walk, plus extra time to eat and play

You'll need: Suitable clothes and footwear; a picnic; map and compass

What's more: The tunnel's only short but it's unlit and the floor is uneven, so take a torch

Grub's up: Croft House Café, Syke Farm Tearoom, Bridge Hotel and Buttermere Court Hotel, all in Buttermere

What's it like?

This might be the most beautiful lakeside walk in the National Park. It passes in and out of woods teeming with wildlife, and along the base of high, rocky fells that loom over us walkers as if we were ants. Waterfalls are part of the experience as are dark, ominous crags. To complete the lake circuit, families have to brave a dark tunnel, and there are also opportunities for paddling, skimming stones and playing Poohsticks.

Grade:
Easy/Moderate

Suitable for:
Children capable of gentle walking for a couple of hours and who don't mind the dark; unsuitable for pushchairs

Family pub

Best friends

Route in a nutshell

Valley track – good lakeside paths along south-west shore, partly through woodland – short section on road – paths rougher, but still relatively easy-going along north-east shore – short unlit tunnel

Fill in each activity on the next page!

ALONG THE WAY

- Skill test ....
- Nature detective ....
- I spy ....
- Cheeky challenge ....

Let's go!

① From the **car park**, head back towards the **Croft House Farm Café** but then bear right along the track beside the **Buttermere Court Hotel**. Ignore a track to Crummock Water branching right.

Go through the gate providing access to the **north-western shore of Buttermere** and turn right. Cross the **footbridge** over the lake's outlet stream, known as **Buttermere Dubs**.

Skill test: Carefully select the best stick to play 'Pooh's game' on the bridge.

② After a **second bridge**, a gate leads into the woods where you pick up the glorious **lakeshore path**. Keep left at any forks, so that you always have uninterrupted views across Buttermere.

The steep, shapely ridge leading up directly from the south-eastern end of the lake is **Fleetwith Edge**.

I spy: Look carefully – can you spot the white cross on the lower slopes of Fleetwith Edge?

Soon after leaving the woods via a small gate, the path crosses **Comb Beck** via a **footbridge**. You're now walking directly beneath some high, rocky fells. It's a dramatic place to be! When a trail heads uphill to the right in a short while, keep left – on the **lower path**.

③ You soon reach a gate and a junction of paths. Turn left through the gate and follow the wide track towards **Gatesgarth Farm**. As you near the buildings, walk along the fenced path to the left of the farmyard.

Adventure 5 | Buttermere ♦ 39

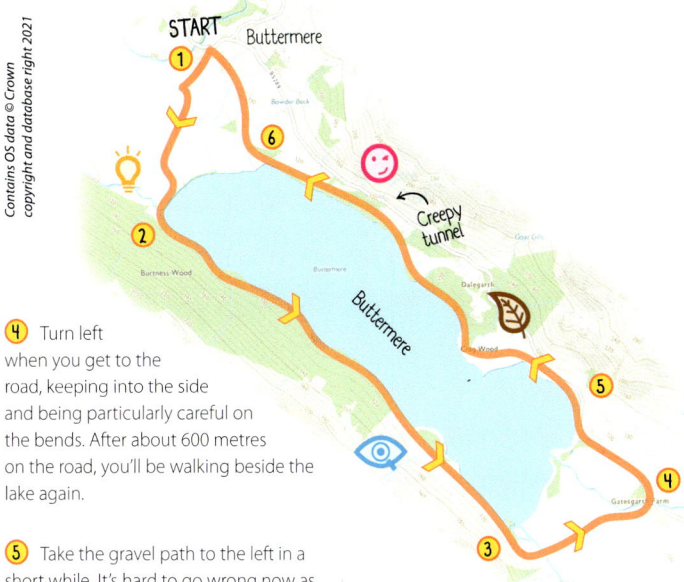

④ Turn left when you get to the road, keeping into the side and being particularly careful on the bends. After about 600 metres on the road, you'll be walking beside the lake again.

⑤ Take the gravel path to the left in a short while. It's hard to go wrong now as the trail makes its way along the lightly **wooded lakeshore,** back towards the village.

> **Nature detective:** Watch for treecreepers scurrying up the tree trunks.

At one point, the path hugs a **shallow ledge** at the base of small, tree-covered crags and then passes through a narrow, **dark tunnel** that's been cut into the rocks.

> **Cheeky challenge:** Do you dare switch off the torch as you walk through the tunnel?

⑥ On reaching the western end of the lake, bear right when the path splits. (The path on the left is closed in spring, while sandpipers nest on the shingle beach.) The path goes through a series of gates and swings up to the right – over rock. At the top of a fenced section, follow the clear path sharp left. It passes some **farm buildings** and a **café** selling home-made ice-cream – an end-of-walk reward perhaps?

At the road, go left and then left again just before the **Bridge Hotel**. Bear right before the **Buttermere Court Hotel** to return to the car park. ♦

💡 Skill test
Poohsticks

Find a stick and **memorise** what it looks like. Then, standing on the side of the **bridge** nearest the **lake**, everyone has to drop their sticks into the water at the same time. **Ready, steady, go...!**

Now cross to the other side of the bridge and wait for the **sticks** to appear below. The first to pass under the **bridge** wins.

On the bridge

Tick your response

- ○ My stick won
- ○ My stick was the slowest
- ○ My stick disappeared

👁 I spy
The cross marks the spot

Look very carefully at the steep ridge, known as **Fleetwith Edge**, leading up from the far end of the lake. On its lower slopes, close to the bottom of the crags, you should be able to make out a **white cross**.

This marks the spot where, in Victorian times, a young woman called **Fanny Mercer** sadly died after tripping and falling from the rocks.

In memory

Tick your response

- ○ Too foggy to see anything
- ○ I can see the ridge but not the cross
- ○ Yes! I can see the cross

Nature detective
Creep up on birds

Treecreepers are small birds that use their long, curved bills to feed on insects that live on the bark of trees. They're hard to spot though because they're mostly **brown**, just like the tree itself. (But they do have white undersides.) If you do see one, it'll probably be clinging to a tree trunk and moving up and around it, in a **dizzying**, spiral fashion.

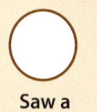

Insect eater

Tick your response

○ Didn't see any   ○ Saw a treecreeper   ○ Saw a tree!

Cheeky challenge
Embrace the dark side!

There are no lights in the **tunnel** and, although it's only short, it gets pretty dark in the middle bit. Are you brave enough to walk through it without a **torch**? Watch your footing though! The floor is uneven and normally has **puddles** in it.

Don't worry if your feel something **slimy** on your head; it's probably just water dripping off the ceiling, but who knows...?

Ooh-er!

Tick your response

○ Needed the torch all the time   ○ I was okay at first, but...   ○ Torch? What's a torch?

42 ♦ Go Wild! In the Lake District

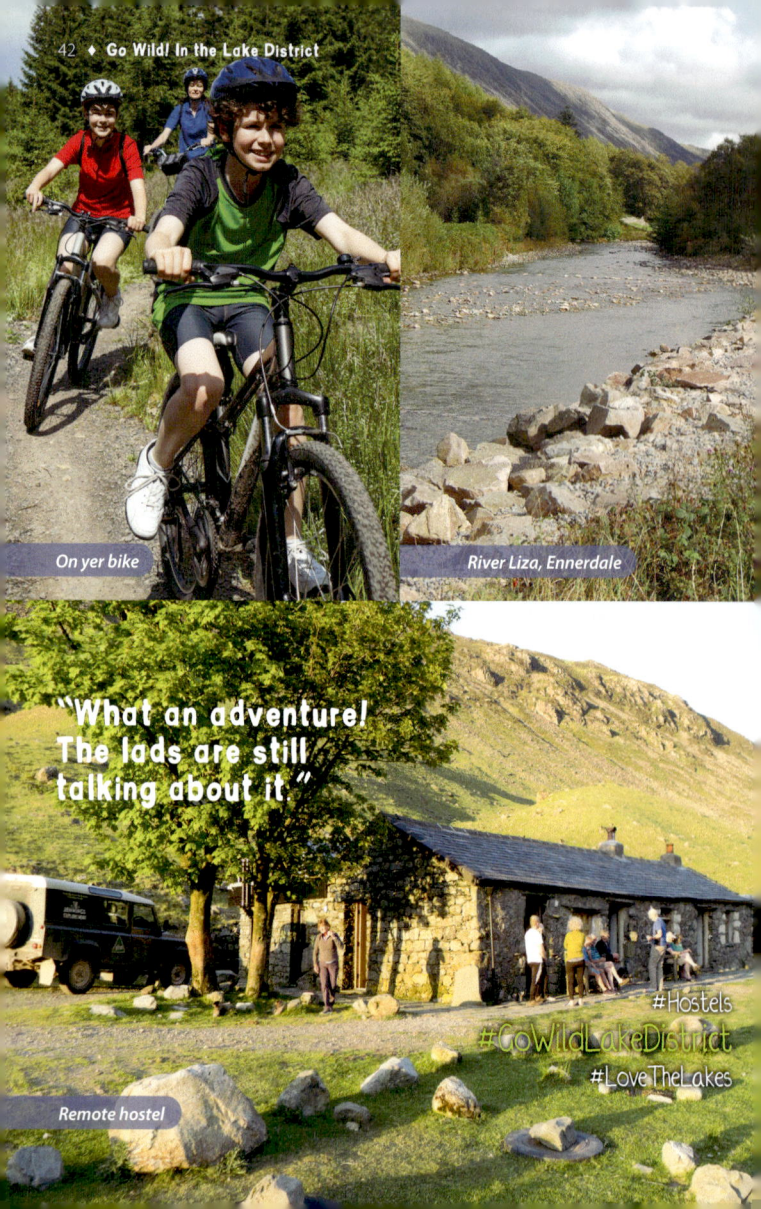

On yer bike

River Liza, Ennerdale

"What an adventure! The lads are still talking about it."

Remote hostel

#Hostels
#GoWildLakeDistrict
#LoveTheLakes

adventure 6

Big bike bash and bunk

Off-road cycle ride with an overnight stay in a remote hostel under the stars

Start: Bowness Knott car park at end of public road on northern shore of Ennerdale Water. OS grid ref: NY 109 153

Map: Ordnance Survey Explorer OL4 (1:25,000), The Lake District: North-western area, *Keswick, Cockermouth & Wigton*

You'll love this if... You enjoy cycling in spectacular mountain scenery and being in wild places at night

How far is it? 5¾ miles/9.5 kilometres (one way)

How long does it take? Overnight adventure. Allow about two hours for the bike ride to Black Sail Hut, and then the same again back the next day

You'll need: Bike and cycling gear, including helmet; clothes and toiletries (and food if self-catering) for an overnight stay; map and compass; torch

What's more: Download a stargazing app before you set off to get the most from your dark-sky experience

Grub's up: You can book meals at Black Sail Hut or use the members' kitchen if you're self-catering

More info: To book bunks at Black Sail Hut, visit the YHA website at **www.yha.org.uk**

Grade:
Moderate

Suitable for:
Families with children capable of cycling for a few hours, and who like the dark

Black Sail Hut

Messing about

What's it like?

With steep-sided fells bounding the valley on either side, woodland teeming with wildlife and no roads to disturb the tranquillity, being in wild Ennerdale is always a wonderful experience; staying here overnight, in one of England's remotest hostels, is even more special. Far from the light pollution of towns and cities, a night spent at Black Sail Hut in this lonely dale is something you won't forget in a hurry.

Route in a nutshell

Valley track, mostly through forest – fairly flat beside lake shore – steady ascent during second half – easy navigation throughout – hostel located beyond trees – retrace route after overnight stay

ALONG THE WAY

Skill test

Nature detective

I spy

Cheeky challenge

Fill in each activity on the next page!

Let's go!

① Leave the **Bowness Knott car park** and turn left along the valley track. This route isn't open to general traffic, so you'll probably not see many vehicles as you head up into the wildest reaches of this peaceful dale – just the occasional four-by-four servicing the handful of buildings here, including two hostels. Before long, you'll be cycling with **Ennerdale Water** on your right. *The prominent crag on the other side of the lake is Anglers' Crag.*

All the while, to the left, the steep slopes are covered in dense woodland. *Take your time – if you stop occasionally, you're more likely to see wildlife in the trees: there are dozens of different bird species here as well as red squirrels scampering about.*

> **Nature detective:** Stop and listen for woodpeckers tapping on tree trunks.

② Having cycled the track for about 2.4 kilometres (1.5 miles), you'll see a track on the right, crossing the **River Liza** close to where it enters **Ennerdale Water**. Ignore this turning; simply keep straight ahead on the main valley track.

Beyond here, you follow the route of **Wainwright's Coast to Coast** long-distance walk, which crosses the country

Adventure 6 | Black Sail Hut ♦ 45

from St Bees on the Irish Sea coast in Cumbria to Robin Hood's Bay on the North Sea Coast in North Yorkshire. *Passing through three spectacular National Parks along the way – the Lake District, the Yorkshire Dales and the North York Moors – it's a whopping 306 kilometres (190 miles) in total, a challenging adventure for families with teenagers. You might find, this evening, that some of the other guests at Black Sail Hut are Coast to Coasters.*

④ At another fork, keep left again, to pass through a gate. It's now just 400 metres (438 yards) to **Black Sail Hut**, where you'll be staying for the night.

Skill test: As the sun goes down, trace the outline of the hills with your finger.

I spy: Once it's dark, go outside, look up and see if you can spot the Milky Way

Contains OS data © Crown copyright and database right 2021

Gentle uphill!

③ When the track splits near the **YHA's Ennerdale hostel** at **High Gillerthwaite**, keep right – along the lower of the two routes. About 310 metres (340 yards) beyond this fork, you'll need to get off your bike to open a **gate** – unless someone else in your party is kind enough to do it for you.

The track has a steady uphill incline as it continues towards the head of the valley. Keep left at the next clear fork and, before long, the trees begin to thin out a bit. *Pillar Rock, on the other side of the valley, is one of Lakeland's most popular climbing crags.*

Black Sail Hut

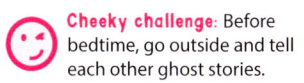

Cheeky challenge: Before bedtime, go outside and tell each other ghost stories.

⑤ The next day, simply cycle back down the valley the way you came – it's much easier on the way back. ♦

Nature detective
Listen for woodpeckers

As you make your way up the valley, stop occasionally and listen for **woodpeckers** tapping on the tree trunks. They might be looking for food (usually insects that live under the bark) or they might be creating a hole in the tree to build a nest in.

Sometimes, **woodpeckers** tap on trees to 'talk' with other woodpeckers.

Tap-tap-tap

Tick your response

○ Didn't hear any!

○ Think we heard one

○ Heard them whenever we stopped

Skill test
'Draw' the hills

As the sun goes down, all you'll see of the surrounding hills is the **outline of their ridges and summits** against the darkening sky. Use your finger to trace the outline of these hills.

The big, dome-like hill looming over the head of the valley is **Great Gable**, one of the most famous fells in the Lake District.

Silhouette of hills

Tick your response

○ Hills covered in cloud

○ Too many midges to sit out

○ Traced the whole ridge!

👁 I spy
Reach for the stars

If you live in a town or city, when you go out at night, you'll only see a few stars. That's because it needs to be **really dark** to see lots of them, and streetlights stop it from getting properly dark. There's hardly any artificial light in Ennerdale though, so, if the sky's clear, you'll see **loads of stars**.

Milky Way

Tick your response

○ Too cloudy for stars

○ There was a full moon

○ Saw the Milky Way!

😉 Cheeky challenge
Spooky stories

Do you know any **ghost stories**? Once it's dark, sit outside the hostel on one of the benches or boulders, and take it in turns to tell **spooky tales**. You've got to get the tone and pace just right if you want to scare your companions.

You might even have some **bats** for company – that'll add to the atmosphere!

Ghost stories

Tick your response

○ Too scared to sit out

○ Managed one story

○ Spent ages scaring each other!

48 ♦ Go Wild! In the Lake District

"There are huge holes. And tunnels. All underground!"

#Caving
#GoWildLakeDistrict
#LakeDistrictUK

Cathedral Cave

Underground explorers

Hodge Close Quarry

adventure 7

Cave and quarry challenge

Clamber through a dramatic landscape riddled with the caves and tunnels of disused quarries

Start: Parking area beside Hodge Close quarry, 5 kilometres north of Coniston. OS grid ref: NY 315 016

Map: Ordnance Survey Explorer OL7 (1:25,000), The Lake District: South-eastern area, *Windermere, Kendal & Silverdale*

You'll love this if... You enjoy messing about in dark holes in the ground and clambering on rock

How far is it? 3½ miles/5.5 kilometres

How long does it take? Half-day adventure. Allow three hours for the route if you're doing all the scrambling

You'll need: Suitable clothes and footwear; a picnic; map and compass; headtorch

What's more: The tunnels have low ceilings and rock falls occasionally occur, so helmets are advisable

Grub's up: The Three Shires Inn, Little Langdale, is on the route

More info: Groups need to keep close together and be aware of the dangers of these quarries, including unstable slopes, sheer drops, deep pools, dark tunnels, slippery rock and rock falls

What's it like?

For the brave, this exploration of the quarries of Little Langdale means donning headtorches and even helmets to scrabble down steep, stony trails, clamber up slimy rock faces and creep along unlit underground tunnels. A less challenging option enables younger families simply to peer into some of the pits and caves as they complete the walk through this pretty part of the Lakes.

Grade:
Hard (moderate if scrambling is bypassed)

Suitable for:
More adventurous families with children confident on rock and happy to explore dark places

Slater Bridge

Helmet on

Route in a nutshell

Optional descent into quarry – woodland track – field paths and quiet lanes – cross unusual, picturesque bridge – visit huge cavern – optional scrambling and tunnel route – good tracks back to start

ALONG THE WAY

Skill test
Nature detective
I spy
Cheeky challenge

Fill in each activity on the next page!

Let's go!

① Walk north-east along the lane. A gap in the fence on the right provides a glimpse into **Hodge Close's main quarry pit**, but keep hold of young children or dogs near the edge.

② Where a track heads right, **signposted 'High Oxen Fell'**, there's a choice. Either ignore the turning and keep straight on, or visit the **quarry pit** and return to this point later. If you choose the latter, as you climb the track, there's a wall on your right. When this ends, a gap in the fence on the right provides access to a stony path that plummets through the trees. After carefully passing through the first pit, you're able to look through **two enormous holes in the slate wall** – straight into the flooded pit you gazed down on earlier.

I spy: Count how many different types of outdoor adventurer you can see.

Retrace your steps to the track junction and continue north-east. The surfaced lane ends at a gate. Once through this, follow a rough track through the woods. Leaving the trees via the next gate, follow the track down to the left. This eventually drops to **Stang End**.

③ Turn left along the surfaced lane and go through the gate on the right – beside the **cottage**. The path leads to a **footbridge over the beck** and then up through a meadow.

④ Turn left along the road. Ignore the first lane on the left as the road climbs beyond the **pub**. In a further 210 metres though, turn left along a farm track.

Adventure 7 | Cathedral Cave ♦ 51

Skill test:
Look at the small lake, or 'tarn', down to the right. What is its name?

When the track swings left, turn right – through a gate. Beyond the next gate, keep close to the wall. The path leads down to **Slater Bridge**, a picturesque old bridge that combines a typical arch-type construction with a clapper bridge, supported by a large boulder mid-stream. Having crossed, climb the wall stile and walk up to a gate. Turn left along the valley track.

5 Nearly 150 metres after a gate across the track, cross the stile beside a locked gate on the right. *It's a good idea to don helmets and get torches ready now.* The track climbs to a flat area and a junction of trails. Ignore the first one, heading uphill; take the next path, which leads, via

Hodge Close Quarry

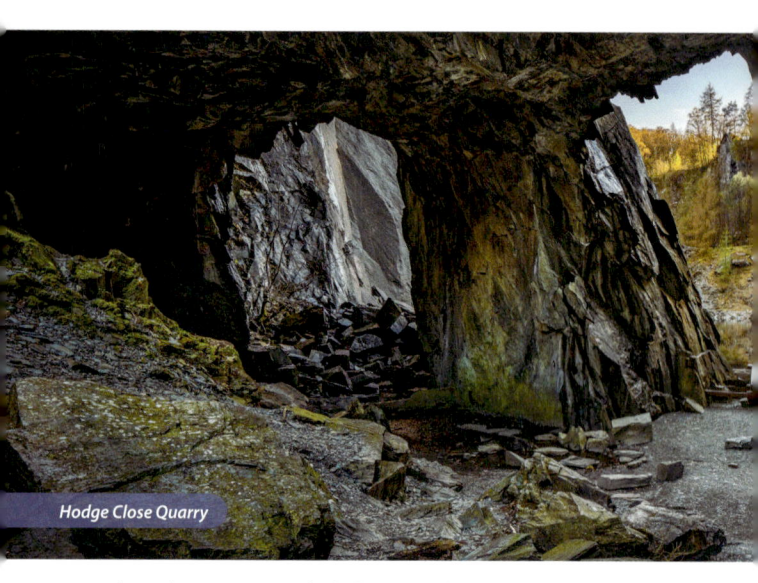

a tunnel, into the impressive **Cathedral Cave**. The roof of the cavern is 12 metres high and there's a massive column of rock in the middle of it.

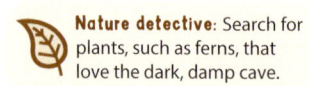

> **Nature detective:** Search for plants, such as ferns, that love the dark, damp cave.

There's another decision to be made now. The simple option descends back to the locked gate, goes right along the valley track and then, on nearing a bridge, turns right again. Bear right at an early fork. You'll rejoin those who braved the quarry route as they re-emerge at a **stile in the low wall** on the right 65 metres beyond the fork.

For the daring though, the adventure continues in **Cathedral Cave**... Beyond the **massive column**, a **short tunnel** can be found below and to the left of the big roof hole.

Once through this, you'll be confronted by a wall of slippery rock. Carefully scale this. At the top, clamber up some more rocks to the base of a sheer wall. You need to follow the **150-metre long tunnel** into this wall, but first switch on your torch because it's completely unlit. Watch your head too; the roof is low. Keep left as a side tunnel heads right.

> **Cheeky challenge:** Do you dare stop and turn your torch off in the total darkness?

Cathedral Cave tunnel

You'll emerge on a **flat area**. A path drops left from here and crosses a stile in a low wall to rejoin those who bypassed the scrambly bits.

6) Turn right along the clear track. When it bends right, take the stony path on the left. Joining with other trails along the way, this route eventually leads back to **Hodge Close**. Turn right along the lane to return to the parking area. ♦

Goldfish bowl?

There have been sightings of goldfish in the large pool in Cathedral Cave, although how they got there remains a mystery. The water is quite deep and murky, so you're not always guaranteed a sighting. Goldfish, which originate from eastern Asia, tend to stay near the bottom of ponds and pools in winter, becoming more active again when the weather warms up in the spring.

👁 I spy
Adventures in the deep

On busy days, you'll see people enjoying all sorts of outdoor activities at **Hodge Close**.

The ladder on the wall to the right is used by **scuba divers** to access the deep pool. There are also several places where, with the help of guides, people **abseil** into the quarry. Can you see any **adventurers** today?

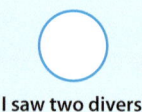

Rock fun

Tick your response

- ○ I saw two divers
- ○ Saw someone abseiling
- ○ We were the only people there

💡 Skill test
Name that tarn

On the way down to Slater Bridge, you'll see a **small lake**, known as a **tarn**, in the valley. Using your map, find its name.

You'll first need to work out exactly where you are and then, with the compass, find out which direction the tarn is in. Other features such as streams and field boundaries might help you.

Tarn-nation

Tick your response

- ○ Is it Ullswater?
- ○ It's Little Langdale Tarn
- ○ I name it Tarny McTarnface!

🍃 Nature detective
Life below

Nature thrives even down here in these **dark, damp quarry pits**. As you wander around Cathedral Cave, particularly if you go through the second tunnel, look for **plants** growing on the slate walls.

These include some **fern** species and various **mosses**. The latter don't have roots; they anchor themselves to the rock using thin cords called 'rhizoids'.

Quarry fern

Tick your response

○ Saw some ferns

○ I touched some soggy moss

○ Didn't see anything

😉 Cheeky challenge
Loving the dark?

Stop for a while in the tunnel and, holding hands with an adult, **turn off your torch**. Although there is one straight section of tunnel where you can see daylight ahead, some sections are totally dark.

Do you dare stand in the **pitch black** while you count to 10? Or maybe you can get all the way to 20? It's scary, isn't it?

Torch dare?

Tick your response

○ I counted to 10

○ I wanted to, but Dad wimped out

○ It was too scary

56 ♦ Go Wild! In the Lake District

Water baby

On the La'al Ratty train

"A steam train AND a waterfall? Wicked!"

#Waterfall
#GoWildLakeDistrict
#LaalRatty

Stanley Ghyll Force

adventure 8

Train trip to a weird waterfall

Catch a miniature train from the coast and walk to a spectacular waterfall in a hidden valley

Start: Dalegarth Station, Boot, Eskdale. OS grid ref: NY 173 007. Catch the La'al Ratty (Ravenglass and Eskdale Railway) from Ravenglass to Dalegarth

Map: Ordnance Survey Explorer OL6 (1:25,000), The Lake District: South-western area, *Coniston, Ulverston & Barrow-in-Furness*

You'll love this if... You love trains, woodland, waterfalls, stepping stones and wildlife

How far is it? 2¾ miles/4.4 kilometres

How long does it take? Full-day adventure. The train trip takes between 60 and 90 minutes (one way). Allow an additional 90 minutes for the walk, plus extra time for rests

You'll need: Some money to pay for the train ride; suitable clothes and footwear; a picnic; map and compass

What's more: Most of the train carriages are open to the elements, so make sure you're prepared for the weather

Grub's up: Fellbites Café at Dalegarth Station; also Brook House Inn and Boot Inn in Boot village

More info: Details of La'al Ratty's fares and timetables at **www.ravenglass-railway.co.uk** or 01229 717171

Grade:
Easy/Moderate

Suitable for:
Families with children capable of easy walking but on rough paths; unsuitable for pushchairs

Café break

Shoulder carry

What's it like?

After a fun journey on the La'al Ratty steam train, from the seaside village of Ravenglass, it's time to explore tranquil Eskdale on foot. First stop is Stanley Ghyll, an atmospheric gorge that is home to the slender ribbon of Stanley Ghyll Force, Lakeland's most magical waterfall. From here, the route heads to the wooded banks of the River Esk, where stepping stones provide excitement for young adventurers and red squirrels watch from the trees.

Route in a nutshell

Short section on quiet lanes – well-constructed, well-signposted valley trails – rougher path in wooded gorge, including stretch on bare rock (can be missed out) – good riverside paths – final section on quiet lanes again

Fill in each activity on the next page!

ALONG THE WAY

Skill test
Nature detective
I spy
Cheeky challenge

Nature detective: Keep your eyes peeled for red squirrels as you explore the valley.

Let's go!

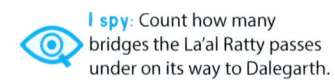

I spy: Count how many bridges the La'al Ratty passes under on its way to Dalegarth.

① From **Dalegarth Station**, turn right along the main valley road. Take the first lane on the left – after about 210 metres. Ignoring the gate giving access to **Parson's Passage** on the left, cross **Trough House Bridge** over some deep pools on the **River Esk**.

② Go through the gate on the left immediately after the bridge – along a path known as **Anne's Walk**.

③ Soon after entering the woods, the gravel path ends close to a fingerpost. To visit **Stanley Ghyll** and its **waterfall**, keep straight on at the fingerpost – climbing the slope over to the right to gain a path beside the wall. (Remember this junction, because you'll return to it after visiting the waterfall.) Soon after some **picnic benches**, a clearer path joins from the right. This heads upstream through a beautiful area of mixed woodland. As you slowly gain height and cross the first **bridge**, the dark woodland slowly closes in around you.

After the **third and final bridge** over the gill, confident walkers will no doubt ignore the signs warning of the steep, slippery path ahead and continue along the side of the cliff to see **Stanley Ghyll Force**, also known as **Dalegarth Force**, in all its glory. But if you're at all nervous or the soles of your footwear don't have good grip on damp rock, it's best to stop at the bridge.

Adventure 8 | Stanley Ghyll ♦ 59

Map labels: START Dalegarth, Boot, Hows Wood, Armont, Eskdale, Choo choo! (1), Beckfoot, Ash Hag, Stepping stones, St Catherine's Church (6), Newhall Coppice (2), (3), (5), Low Wood, Force Wood, Cool forests, Waterfall (4)

Contains OS data © Crown copyright and database right 2021

4 From here, retrace your steps to the fingerpost at the crossing of paths near to where Anne's Walk ended (waypoint three). Remember to ignore any paths to the left on your walk back downstream.

Turn right at the fingerpost – signposted 'Gill Force and Doctor Bridge'. Cross a **footbridge** and continue to a gate. Once through it, ignore the clear track heading right; instead, keep straight on – along the edge of the trees. You'll soon see some **stepping stones** over the River Esk (through a gate on the left).

Cheeky challenge: Are you brave enough to cross the stepping stones and then come back?

On the La'al Ratty steam train

Continue along the **river's south bank**. In a few more metres, before the path narrows, fork right to continue in the same direction but now at a higher level, beside a fence. After the next gate, the path climbs slightly. Watch for a waymarker post indicating a sharp bend to the right. This is quickly followed by a junction where you turn sharp left.

> **Skill test:** Use your map to locate the source of the River Esk, high up in the Lakeland fells.

(5) Cross the **River Esk** via the **bridge** over a narrow, rocky gorge and then head downstream. At a choice of two gates, go through the one on the left, continuing towards **St Catherine's Church**. (If you carry on until you draw level with the far end of the church, you'll see the stepping stones again.)

There's a spooky story associated with this little church... In the time before Wasdale had a graveyard, coffins used to be carried on horseback across the bleak moors to be buried here at St Catherine's. On one stormy day, the horse carrying the coffin of a young man suddenly took fright and disappeared on Eskdale Moor. When the dead man's mother heard her son's body had been lost, the shock proved too much and she died. While mourners were transporting her coffin to Eskdale, they hit bad weather and, again,

Adventure 8 | Stanley Ghyll

Local sign

the horse bolted. It was never seen again, although some say you can sometimes still hear hoofbeats on the moor when the fog descends.

⑥ At the **church**, turn right along the lane. When you reach the road – opposite the **Brook House Inn** – turn left. **Dalegarth Station** is on the right in 230 metres. ♦

Red alert!

Watch for red squirrels in woods and along woodland edges, particularly where there's a mixture of broadleaf and conifer trees. Contrary to popular belief, they don't hibernate, although they're less likely to be out and about if the weather's cold, wet or windy. Autumn's a good time to spot them because that's when they're busy hiding food away to keep them going through the winter.

👁 I spy
A bridge too far...?

The **Ravenglass and Eskdale Railway**, affectionately known locally as the **La'al Ratty**, was originally built to carry iron ore from the mine at Boot to the main railway line at Drigg.

As you travel from Ravenglass to Dalegarth, count **how many bridges** you pass under. If you lose count, don't forget you'll get a second go at it on the way back.

Tiny train

Tick your response

- Counted seven
- Got a different total on each journey
- Lost count!

🍃 Nature detective
Red squirrels

There used to be **red squirrels** all over Britain but the Lake District is one of the few places where you'll see them now in England.

These cute, fluffy-tailed creatures, smaller than grey squirrels, live in trees, so watch out for them running along branches. You might also spot them on walls. **Pine cones** are one of their favourite snacks, so **chewed cones** are a sign squirrels live in the area.

Nuts, whole hazelnuts ...

Tick your response

- Spotted a squirrel!
- Saw some chewed cones
- Didn't see anything!

Cheeky challenge
Stepping stones

You'll need a good sense of balance and a little bit of bravery to cross the **stepping stones** across the River Esk. (Don't attempt it if the water level is anywhere near the top of the stones though.)

If you're not sure you're up to it, you'll get a second chance at it later in the route after you've crossed to the other side of the river and reached St Catherine's Church.

Wet or dry?

Tick your response

- ◯ I was too nervous
- ◯ River was too high
- ◯ Yay! I did it!

Skill test
Find the source

The **river** you're walking beside is the **Esk**. It's about 27 kilometres (17 miles) long, and gets wider and slower as it nears the sea.

Find out where you are on the map and then follow the blue line of the river upstream (away from the sea) back to where it starts (its **source**). A clue... It starts high in the hills and then flows downhill.

Eskdale

Tick your response

- ◯ It starts on Hardknott Pass
- ◯ It starts on Esk Pike
- ◯ Got confused by all the blue lines!

64 ♦ Go Wild! In the Lake District

"We had a lovely day for our bike ride with the kids. The views across the lake were amazing!"

#Adventure
#GoWildLakeDistrict
#Windermere

Wooded Windermere shore

Let's go!

Café in the Courtyard

adventure 9

Ferry and lakeshore bike ride

Take bikes on the boat across Windermere to cycle on the traffic-free shore path

Start : Bark Barn Jetty, near Belle Grange on Windermere's west shore. OS grid ref: SD 388 988. Bring bikes across on the summer-only Bike-Boat service from Brockhole

Map: Ordnance Survey Explorer OL7 (1:25,000), The Lake District: South-eastern area, *Windermere, Kendal & Silverdale*

You'll love this if... You enjoy boat trips and lakeside cycling through tranquil woods

How far is it? 4½ miles/7 kilometres (there and back, but can be cut short at any point)

How long does it take? Half-day adventure. Allow up to three hours for the cycle ride. The boat trip takes 15 minutes each way

You'll need: A bike; suitable clothes, including a bike helmet; food and drink; map and compass

What's more: Children on single-gear bikes might have to get off and push on some uphill sections

Grub's Up: Café in the Courtyard at Claife Viewing Station

More info: For details on the Windermere Lake Cruises' Bike-Boat, visit www.windermere-lakecruises.co.uk or phone 015394 43360. To hire bikes from the visitor centre at Brockhole on Windermere, visit **www.brockhole.co.uk** or phone 015394 46601

What's it like?

Cycling along Windermere's wooded, western shore is a tranquil affair. There's a good, broad, traffic-free track for most of the way from Bark Barn to the turning point near The Ferry House. The last 1.5 kilometres is on a narrow lane, but even this sees few cars. There are some uphill sections, but they're relatively short and gentle. If anyone's getting tired, you can turn back at any point on the route.

Grade:
Easy/Moderate

Suitable for:
Younger families just getting into cycling

Claife viewing station

Boys on bikes

Route in a nutshell

Beyond jetty, off-road track leads south along wooded shore – some uphill bits – one steep (but short) downhill stretch – after crossing cattle grid, short section on surfaced lane – retrace route

ALONG THE WAY

Skill test
Nature detective
I spy
Cheeky challenge

Fill in each activity on the next page!

Let's go!

① After getting off the boat at **Bark Barn**, wheel your bike along the **jetty** and around the side of the small building. Once you're clear of the other passengers, you can start pedalling. Don't be tempted by the path heading up to the right immediately after the Bark Barn information board; instead, keep left and then turn left along the clear track. It's fairly level at first and you're close to the lake, so you can see through the trees to the opposite shore.

Cheeky challenge: Are you good enough for the balance beam?

② When the short stretch of wall on your right ends, the track climbs slightly. If you find it a bit hard, take some time to rest and enjoy the **peaceful woodland**.

Nature detective: Look around and count how many different tree species you can see.

③ After another **uphill section**, you'll see a wall on your left. You've got a **steep downhill** section ahead of you now. It's only short, but if you're at all nervous about it or you're not used to your bike, you might want to get off and wheel your bike down. If you cycle it, be careful of the loose stones and the bumpy bits of bare rock.

④ You'll eventually see another track going up to the right. Ignoring this, keep straight ahead, quickly crossing a **cattle grid**. You're now on a smoother, **surfaced**

Adventure 9 | Windermere Shore ♦ 67

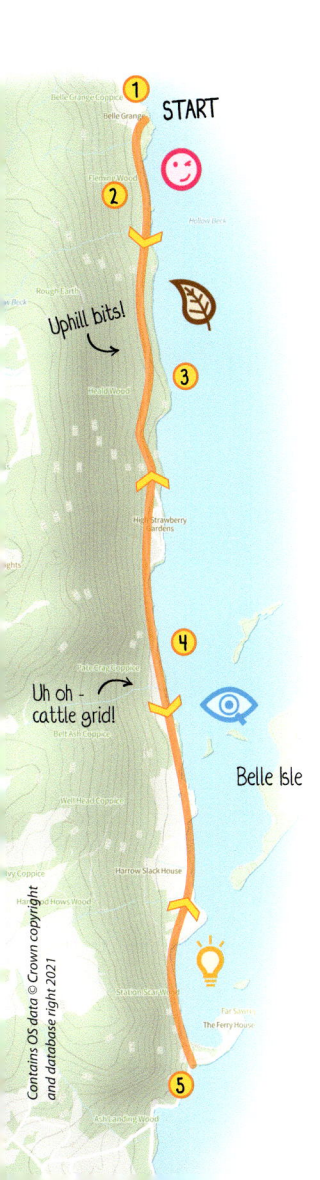

lane and, although there's still not much traffic, you're more likely to encounter cars now, so be careful.

Before long, the trees on your left part to reveal some beautiful views across **Windermere**. At just over 18 kilometres long, this is England's largest natural lake.

I spy: Look out on the water and count how many sail boats you can see.

As the lane becomes a little more enclosed, you'll see the **Café in the Courtyard** through a stone archway on the right – a good place for a rest and a treat if you're lucky.

5 When you reach a T-junction with a road, it's time to turn round and head back to Bark Barn the way you came. (Alternatively, if you turn left here, you could get the ferry across Windermere and then cycle back to Brockhole, but most of this is on busy roads.)

As you head back along the shore path, you're treated to some great views of the mountains beyond the top end of the lake.

Skill test: Try taking one hand off the handlebars to wave at other people on the track.

Some time after crossing the cattle grid, as you head deeper into the woods, remember to watch for the track down to **Bark Barn** on your right. ♦

Cheeky challenge
Sticky bit?

Place **two lines of sticks**, parallel with each other, on a flat, straight bit of track. Start with them about 25 centimetres apart, and see if you can **cycle straight through the gap** between them.

Once you've done it, **try shrinking the gap** between the two lines of sticks. It'll be harder now to keep your balance.

Between the sticks

Tick your response

25cm was easy | 15cm! Result! | I tried 10cm but fell off

Nature detective
Tree total

There are lots of **different types of trees** in the woodland beside Windermere, including beech, sycamore, sweet chestnut, hazel, oak, birch, various conifers and even the occasional ancient yew.

Stop and see **how many different species** you can count. The easiest way to spot the various types is to **look at their leaves**. They're all different.

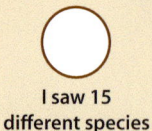

Mixed leaves

Tick your response

I counted 3 | I saw 15 different species | Trees all look the same to me

I spy
Lots of yachts

There are **sailing boats** of all different shapes and sizes on Windermere. Some are just small dinghies suitable for one or two sailors to mess about in; others are bigger yachts with cabins below deck where people can sleep.

There are motor boats out there too, but you're looking for sailing boats – the ones with the tall masts.

Sailing boats

Tick your response

○ Saw two, but none with their sails up

○ Lost count

○ Too foggy to see anything

Skill test
Give us a wave!

Now you're getting used to your bike, **try taking one hand off the handlebars** to wave at other people on the track – walkers or other cyclists.

Like the cheeky challenge earlier, you'll need good balance to do this. It's best to wait until you're on a fairly flat section without too many bumpy bits.

Hands off

Tick your response

○ I waved at everyone I saw

○ I managed a little wave

○ I tried but I fell off

70 ♦ Go Wild! In the Lake District

Downhill skills

Ready to roll

#Grizedale
#GoWildLakeDistrict
#LakesMTB

"I was nervous on the downhill bit, but it was great fun in the end."

Follow the leader

adventure 10

Forest monster biking

Thrilling mountain biking on trails among the trees in Lakeland's biggest forest

Start: Main Grizedale Forest car park, a few hundred metres south of visitor centre. OS grid ref: SD 336 941

Map: Ordnance Survey Explorer OL7 (1:25,000), The Lake District: South-eastern area, *Windermere, Kendal & Silverdale*

You'll love this if... You love cycling among the trees, far from the noise and fumes of the traffic

How far is it? 6½ miles/10.4 kilometres (shorter version, 3¾ miles/5.9 kilometres)

How long does it take? Full-day adventure. Allow about three or four hours for the long cycle ride, plus extra time for rests

You'll need: A bike; suitable clothes, including a bike helmet; food and drink; map and compass

What's more: Because there's a lot of uphill riding, this route isn't suitable for children on single-gear bikes

Grub's Up: Café at Grizedale Forest Visitor Centre

More info: To hire bikes from the visitor centre, visit **www.grizedalemountainbikes.co.uk** or phone 01229 860335. Broad range available including children's bikes, tag-a-longs, trailers and, for those over 14, e-bikes

Grade:
Hard (with moderate option)

Suitable for:
Older or more confident families who can manage off-road cycling with sustained uphill work

What's it like?

Grizedale Forest is a sprawling area of woodland covering the rolling hills between Windermere and Coniston Water. It's home to miles of tracks and trails suitable for off-road cyclists of all abilities – from families to hardened trail riders. This route keeps to wide, well-maintained forest tracks as it climbs from broad-leaved woods to conifer plantation. There's a long climb in the first half, but less experienced cyclists can cut the route short.

In gear

Cycle track

Route in a nutshell

After crossing road and cycling along farm lane, it's all off road – broad forestry tracks – lots of uphill work in first half – downhill on narrower tracks – good views on highest part of the route – occasional art installations

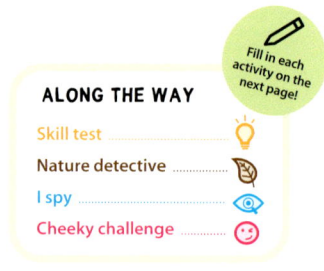

ALONG THE WAY

- Skill test
- Nature detective
- I spy
- Cheeky challenge

Fill in each activity on the next page!

Let's go!

1 Head to the top of the **car park**, keeping close to the wall beside the road, and continue to a gap in the wall. Cross the road and cycle along the **lane opposite**, beside the visitor centre. Drawing level with **farm buildings** on the right, turn left through some gates. A broad track heads up towards the **forest**.

2 After a cattle grid, bear left along a **wide forest track** – following the green and orange cycle routes for now. After about 1.1 kilometres on this track, you'll see a path dropping left. Ignore this but then bear right at a fork. There's a long, steady ascent now – through oak woods initially.

3 The gradient briefly eases as the track swings left to cross Farra Grain. As it begins climbing again, ignore a narrower route to the left; keep to the broad track as it bends right. The woodland is now dominated by conifers – trees that produce leaves that look like needles.

Skill test: Collect some conifer cones to use for a target-practice game.

4 At a junction, turn right – following just the **orange cycle route** now.

5 On reaching the next junction, there's a choice: the main route goes left, or, for the shorter version, turn right. If you choose the latter, you might need to wheel your bike down some steeper sections. (The short version rejoins the main route at waypoint 8 [wp8]).

Adventure 10 | Grizedale Forest ♦ 73

I spy: Soon after the junction, watch for the 'Treefold' to the right of the main route.

After a **bench**, you'll see a path on the left which leads on to **Carron Crag**, the highest point in the forest, but this is for walkers only.

After passing a track on the left, you begin your downhill journey. Keep to the main track until, immediately after another route joins from the left, it splits in two.

6 Bear right here – signed **Moor Top**.

Nature detective: Look for critters in a pool about 230 metres after junction.

At the next clear junction, as the main track bends left, keep straight on – leaving the orange route. The path's steep and loose at times, so you might want to wheel your bike down.

7 At the bottom of this drop, turn right, following the **green and purple bike trails**.

Cheeky challenge: See who can cycle the slowest. (Not as easy as it sounds!)

8 About 2.3 kilometres along this track, cyclists doing the short version rejoin the main route. (As they drop on to the main track, they'll need to turn right.) In a further 420 metres, having ignored narrower paths, take a broad track on the left. (There are posts either side with waymarker symbols on them.) This crosses a cattle grid which you'll recognise from earlier. Now retrace your route to the car park. ♦

Skill test
Pine cone bullseye

Using a stick, mark out **three circles** on an area of flat, bare ground. They need to be concentric (one inside the other).

Now collect a handful of **pine cones**. Making sure you're all standing the same distance from the circles, throw your **pine cones** into them to see who can get closest to the inner circle.

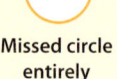

Woodland game

Tick your response

○ Missed circle entirely
○ Reached outer circle
○ Bullseye!

I spy
Forest art

'Treefold: Centre' is one of many **sculptures** and other **artistic creations** in the forest. Harriet and Rob Fraser used dry-stone walling techniques to build this neat, circular fold containing a single aspen tree.

Several of the stones are **carved with words** that combine with two other 'treefolds' in Cumbria – near Ullswater and on Little Asby Common – to make up a poem.

One, two, three

Tick your response

○ We couldn't find it
○ Found it
○ Want to read the rest of the poem now!

🍃 Nature detective
Pond life

There are **small pools** throughout the forest that are home to weird and wonderful creatures. About 230 metres after the junction to 'Moor Top', look to the left of the track for one of these **ponds**.

You might see **water boatmen** paddling on the surface of the **pool** or even colourful **dragonflies** darting about.

Dragonfly

Tick your response
- ◯ Didn't see anything!
- ◯ Saw a big, blue dragonfly
- ◯ Spotted all sorts of stuff

🙂 Cheeky challenge
Slow bike ride

Find a reasonably flat, straight section of track. Decide on a starting point and a finish line. (You could mark them with sticks – beside the track, not across it.)

Now, instead of seeing who's the first to reach the finish line, see **who can be last**. It's really hard to **cycle slowly** without losing your balance!

Slow 'n' easy

Tick your response
- ◯ I fell off!
- ◯ I was the fastest
- ◯ I was the slowest

Formal/paid activities

Brockhole: *Activities include TreetopTrek and TreetopNets, boat and bike hire, orienteering courses and archery.* Brockhole, Windermere, LA23 1LJ | www.brockhole.co.uk | 015394 46601 | info@brockhole.co.uk

Coniston Boating Centre: *Hire of bikes, paddle boards, kayaks, canoes and rowing boats on Coniston Water.* Lake Road, Coniston, LA21 8AN | www.conistonboatingcentre.co.uk | 015394 41366 | conistonbc@lakedistrict.gov.uk

Go Ape: *Tree-top adventures including obstacle courses and zip-lines at two Lake District locations – Whinlatter and Grizedale. Segway tours also available.* www.goape.co.uk | 01603 895500

Rookin House: *Multi-activity centre, including archery, horse-riding, assault course and fishing.* Rookin House Farm, Ullswater CA11 0SS | www.rookinhouse.co.uk | 017684 83561 | enquiries@rookinhouse.co.uk

Alpacaly Ever After: *Walks with alpacas and llamas, lasting between 1½-8 hours. Various locations in northern Lake District.* www.alpacalyeverafter.co.uk | 017687 78328 | info@alpacalyeverafter.co.uk

West Lakes Adventure: *Guided outdoor adventures including rock climbing, canoeing and raft building. Mostly Eskdale and Wasdale.* www.westlakesadventure.co.uk | 019467 23753 | enquiries@westlakesadventure.co.uk

Lowther Castle: *Ruins, gardens, bike hire and The Lost Castle adventure playground.* Lowther Castle, near Penrith, CA10 2HH | www.lowthercastle.org | 01931 712192 | info@lowthercastle.org

Useful information ♦ 77

Honister Slate Mine: *Underground tours of slate mine and outdoor via ferrata adventures.* Honister Pass, Borrowdale, Keswick CA12 5XN | **www.honister.com** | 017687 77230 | info@honister.com

Lakeland Maze Farm Park: *Maize maze, farm animals, trampolines and go-karts.* Raines Hall, Sedgwick, Kendal, LA8 0JH | **www.lakelandmaze.co.uk** | 015395 61760 | info@lakelandmaze.co.uk

Lake District Wildlife Park: *Exotic animals, bird of prey displays and play areas (indoor and outdoor).* Lake District Wildlife Park, Bassenthwaite, CA12 4RD | **www.lakedistrictwildlifepark.co.uk** | 01768 776239

Muncaster Castle: *Haunted castle, gardens, play areas, maze and bird of prey displays.* Muncaster Castle, Ravenglass, CA18 1RD | **www.muncaster.co.uk** | 01229 717614 | info@muncaster.co.uk

Park Foot Pony Trekking: *Off-road pony treks (up to 1½ hours) for all abilities.* Howtown Road, Pooley Bridge, Penrith, CA10 2NA | **www.ponytrekkingullswater.co.uk** | 017684 86696 | parkfootponytrekking@gmail.com

Keswick Adventures: *Family-friendly activities such as paddle boarding, ghyll scrambling and canoeing. Mostly North Lakes* | **www.keswickadventures.co.uk** | 07712 162088 | info@keswickadventures.co.uk

Wet weather/indoor adventures

Ambleside Climbing Wall: *Taster sessions and private lessons for ages six and up.* Ambleside Adventure, 101 Lake Road, Ambleside LA22 0DB | **www.amblesideadventure.co.uk** | 015394 33794 | info@amblesideadventure.co.uk

Keswick Climbing Wall: *Indoor sessions include 'kids climbing hour' and 'family fun hour'.* Goosewell Farm, Keswick, CA12 4RN | **www.activity-centre.com** | 017687 72000 | info@activity-centre.com

Wray Castle: *Creative play for younger families in a Gothic Revival castle beside Windermere.* Low Wray, Ambleside, LA22 0JA | **www.nationaltrust.org.uk** | 01539 433250 | wraycastle@nationaltrust.org.uk

World of Beatrix Potter: *Beatrix Potter's best-loved characters are brought to 3D life for young families.* Crag Brow, Bowness-on-Windermere, LA23 3BX | **www.hop-skip-jump.com** | 015394 88444

Keswick Museum: *Lots of fun and informative exhibits, suitable for children and adults alike. Café on site.* Station Road, Keswick, CA12 4NF | **www.keswickmuseum.org.uk** | 017687 73263

Windermere Jetty: *Boating museum where kids' activities include dressing-up and model boat sailing.* Rayrigg Road, Bowness-on-Windermere, LA23 1BN | **www.lakelandarts.org.uk** | 01539 637940 | info@windermerejetty.org

Puzzling Place: *Optical illusions that will fool your eyes and brain, including holograms and balls rolling uphill.* Museum Square, Keswick, CA12 5DZ | **www.puzzlingplace.mobi** | 017687 75102